WING WHISPERINGS

In our acts of conservation
we revere and pay homage
to nature's magnificence

Eric Hellman
9/05

WING
WHISPERINGS

C. Eric Hellmann

Edited by Barbara Humberger

ᗡP

Aventine Press

Published by Aventine Press
1202 Donax Ave Suite 12
Imperial Beach, CA 91932, USA
www.aventinepress.com

ISBN: 1-59330-162-6
Printed in the United States of America

To my Mother, "Annie" Hellmann. The woman of
wisdom who showed me the beauty of life,
then taught me the words to describe it.

Epigraph

"Every artist dips his brush in his own soul, and paints his own nature into his pictures."

--- Henry Ward Beecher

Contents

List of Illustrations

Foreword

Welcome to a hunter's world! Many of the poems in this collection are about nature, conservation, and my obsession with hunting in the wild outdoors. Other selections are very personal and reflective. The pursuit of my sport was severely curtailed in 1995 when I became completely disabled with Chronic Fatigue and Fibromyalgia. Only through the supportive efforts of my friends and fellow hunters at the Oak Harbor Conservation Club was I able to continue my involvement with the shooting sports and in conservation activities. I will be eternally grateful for their friendship and help.

Acknowledgements

My many thanks to my editor, Barbara Humberger, who continually encouraged my efforts, and corrected my creative grammar.

My thanks to Todd Hollis of the Associated Press International for permission to use his moving picture of the World Trade Center Crash (ref: signature # 5976033). Used here as: "World Trade Center, September 11, 2001".

My thanks to my old friend Denny Van Wey, Assistant Police Chief of Fremont, OH who contributed two pictures that he took of the aftermath of the destruction of the World Trade Center. Shown in this book as: "Standing Tall At WTC", and "The Bones of Innocence". A special thanks to all the police and fire departments of Ohio who sent many of their members, like Denny, to assist their brothers-in-grief in the efforts to clean up the site and retrieve our fallen citizens.

I am eternally grateful for Nancy, my cherished partner in love and life.

Introduction

When hunters and fisherman pursue their sport, they are extremely cognizant of their surroundings. The final outcome of their quest is determined by their depth of knowledge of the game they pursue, and the sportsman's ability to read the finite changes in the habitat and weather. A successful outdoorsman is always a gifted observer who can fully appreciate the majesty and grandeur of America's wild outdoors. The observation and perception skills that we learn while seeking our quarry are readily transferable to all our real-life experiences. Hunters become the quintessential seekers.

Gift

This land once bred but quiet men
Who lived on corn and pemmican.
Their Maker dwelt in earth and trees,
Within the beasts, the sun, the breeze.
They roamed at will this grand expanse,
Revering things beheld by chance.

In age we came to civilize,
Their sacred trusts, we compromised.
As modern man we've grown complex
And hung our faith around their necks.
We masters of this savaged land,
Now heathens of the Maker's plan.

Deep in our souls we know it's wrong
When daily grind mutes nature's song.
Our skills and will can not suffice
To supercede earth's natural life.
We must take care of where we dwell,
This precious gift 'tween Heaven and Hell.

Canada Goose
Magee Marsh

Hunting Dance

From reed wrapped blind
    I stole a glance,
        At a flight of geese
            on which I chanced.
They picked their way
    through blustery skies,
        To assault my pond
            where decoys lie.
Whispering wind
    on wood shaved reed,
        Produce the calls
            that the fliers heed.
With throaty honks
    they beg to land . . .
        Unseen I crouch
            in Pampas stand.
Cupped wings arrest
    their southbound flight,
        And thrash the air
            with all their might.
They drop like leaves
    from some great tree,
        They slide and turn,
            then drop with ease.
Webbed feet extend
    to navigate,
        This deathly dervish
            becomes their fate.
Resounding blasts
    take one, then two,
        The dance now ends,
            the encore's through.

World Trade Center
September 11, 2001

9111

Gleaming Gemini of glass and steel
that graced the Gotham shore,
Wellspring of wealth and commerce
for the Republic which it bore.

Undisputed money Mecca,
the great capital of coin,
Willing sanctuary for the scoundrels
when fat profits were purloined.

Dreamers mundane destination,
gamblers giant Monaco,
Where market machinations
persuade faint-hearted not to go.

Rampart of fiscal fortress,
singular symbol of "The Street",
Where the bottom line of good and bad
of our economy meet.

Now the wicked and the worldly,
mix with Samaritans and saints,
Many innocents were sacrificed,
on terror's altar of complaints.

Exploding arrows of assassins
that tumbled towers down
In an act of criminal cunning,
no more vile can be found.

Beware malevolent monsters,
from the ashes we will arise,
To take a fearsome measure
for the many who have died.

With death and great destruction,
you sought to bring us low,
But you raised us from complacent sleep,
our great resolve to show.

You have brought us all together,
Hindu, Muslim, Christian, Jew,
To gain justice for the nations
of the victims that you slew.

Today we rise together
as the polyglot we are,
White, yellow, black and brown men
will pursue you near and far.

As we gather your fanatics
and your dreams they turn to dust,
You'll rue the day you came here...
or that you ever messed with us.

Tundra Swans
Dr. L.J. Darr Memorial Wetland

The Royals

With majestic form and beauty
They've graced our northern pond,
A tableau etched in ivory bisque
These elegant tundra swans.

Strutting monarchs of the marshland
Courtly in their gliding flow,
They've come to rest, perhaps to nest,
On secluded tracts where cygnets grow.

The serene marsh absorbs the richness
Of their infrequent mellow calls,
Wrapped in spectrums of bold colors
When sun sets and evening falls.

Come the Fall they'll float above us
Taking migration further south,
Woven through resplendent tapestry
Hung above the river's mouth.

Kronauge's Kill
John Kronauge, Kurt Hellmann, and Drake.
John and Drake's first pheasant.

The Savage

Blood-red moon of early winter
This morn' hangs on marshland crest.
In distant past it called the red men,
Bent upon their vengeful quest.

But in this time of new millennia,
The only warriors you might see
Are the legions of the hunters
Among the cattails, or cloaked by trees.

In war paint of thermal camo
And equipped with high tech gear,
In pursuit of wild creatures
As they range both far and near.

The tools of death now differ greatly,
But the obsession's quite the same.
Deep within still burns the passion
That drove the myriad sons of Cain.

Some will see the hunt as blood sport
And bemoan the loss of life,
But the stirrings of the savage
Have been with me all my life.

The Looking Glass

When gazing in the mirror
Hoping finally to see through,
Always searching for the better me
Or some guy I once knew.

Can't dwell upon shortcomings,
Or the great beauty that I lack,
Or stand aghast at bungled past
Pursuing youth that won't come back.

Is this visage of light and shadows
All that others will perceive?
Or will I bestow some inner glow
For my fellows to receive?

When I get past the painted glass
And reflect in some soul's face,
It's there I'll tell if I'll burn in hell
Or be consumed by heavenly grace.

Great White and Black Crowned Heron
Dr. L.J. Darr Memorial Wetland

First Light

Come dawn my world's secluded
In frieze of fixed phragmites screen,
From the innards of my duck blind
The waking marshland can be seen.

Unobserved by stealthy heron
That on barren deadfalls rest,
I'll chance a glance at darting killdeer
Come to feed on mudflat's crest.

Entertained by cruising muskrat
Intent on weaving winter hutch,
To these teaming marshland creatures,
My unknown presence doesn't count for much.

I'll stay still and counsel patience
Deep within this shooter's womb,
In hopes my tempting decoy spread
Will attract the dabblers soon.

Awaiting moment of decision
When mallards cup their graceful wings,
Trusting luck and steady shooting
This morn' will cause my soul to sing.

Victors

History's but a roadmap
that most mortals seldom heed.
Great knowledge crammed in volumes
that students fail to read.

Distilled of hard-taught lessons,
some of triumph, some of pain.
Once lived and dearly paid for,
that we're sure to learn again.

Grand stories of great heroes,
common men like you and me,
who emerged from desperation
to bring tyrants to their knees.

It's not the kings and all their generals
who leave their names upon the rocks,
nor rich merchants with their markets,
or fat bankers with their stocks.

Mighty empires have expired,
time has laid false prophets low.
In the ground great legends molder,
over time not much to show.

All before is dead and passing,
all the grandeur's 'neath the dust,
all things that are worth saving
we keep inside of us.

What works becomes the present
as we go about our lives,
for the victors of the history are we ...
just common guys.

Mallard Hen and Family
Sandusky River

Ducky Dues

Some days it's raining mallards,
other days it's snowing geese.
Most days when I go hunting
it's just to find some peace.

With all the bloody effort
that I put into this sport,
I hope my pond for dabblers
won't be their last resort.

Long months of preparation,
sacrifice and great expense,
When I tally season's game bag
this addiction makes poor sense.

It's no sport for fine day hunters,
damn hard work is what's in store,
When first dawn arrived in sunshine
crusty duckmen cursed and swore.

All the planting and the pumping,
and the patching rutted dikes,
And lying out in freezing rains
that all waterfowl seem to like.

Repainted deeks of wood'n cork
raft on the workshop floor,
Daydreams of hopeful hunters
conjure up fat flocks galore.

There seems no earthly limit
to the effort I put in,
Even though flocks are infrequent
and the shootin's mighty thin.

First week was fair-to-middl'n,
all the boys got one or two,
And we're hope'n skies turn blustery
before mid-season's through.

To my blind of wood and cattails
the morning pilgrimage I'll make,
And trust from this migration
many ducks and geese I'll take.

Just how many future seasons
will I climb into this blind?
For my fervent quest of waterfowl,
slows only pace of life – not time.

Footnotes

When future generations
peruse the book of life,
will they find my page uncluttered,
or with accomplishments be rife?

Might it be consoling reading
of a time that's been well spent?
Or replete with errant stories
of the sins I must repent?

Will it speak of great adventure
and a life that's well explored?
Or just list my dismal failures,
and the multitudes that I've bored?

Is it an ode to personal sacrifice
offered up for all mankind?
Might it suggest I'm self-possessed,
and to others needs' quite blind?

If craving humble footnote
for last line that may be penned,
say I went to God believing,
it's the beginning not the end.

Titans

December landscape on the river
turns to many shades of brown,
Long gone the vibrant colors
that in the Fall abound.

Still there are great things of beauty
for those inclined to see,
As Nature works her wonders,
on stark and barren trees.

On the canvas of a pearl-gray sky,
each branch is layered in
While the textures of imposing trunks
run from coarse to pencil thin.

Wrapped in hues across the spectrum
from the ever-changing light,
Surrealistic shifting shadows come,
stretching tones from black to white.

Gnarled roots grip as if determined,
the wet ground beneath their feet.
Under woody limbs stand knots of grass,
as summer blades retreat.

Soft moist mats of growing lichen
decorate trunk's northern face.
On cracked and rotting old spars,
hanging vines weave death's embrace.

These sleeping giants of the Summer
punctuate the river's banks,
Cradled in soft beds of cattail
as they straddle steep dike flanks.

Marching out to far horizon,
bordering switchgrass fields around,
Offset by stands of conifers
that prefer the drier ground.

They'll stand like that all Winter;
darn near death, or so it seems.
With the passing of late season's snows,
they define what rebirth means.

In the flows of early Springtime
with the rambling river's tide,
Deep within the twisted titans,
will the surging sap arise.

When new buds grace barren branches
and the grass turns pastel green,
All the promise of the Summer shows
in each new sprout that's seen.

Once again these dancing beauties
are ushered in by grand design,
For it's the promise of the Coming,
that has met the test of time.

Surge

When love was young I strode this shore
Of rocks and glistening sand,
To leave my marks of higher tides
In sweet pleasure, and conquests grand.

Old loves were met on windy quays
To quench hot summer lusts,
But the passions of my younger years
Have long since turned to dust.

Painful longings to reclaim those days
And relive high times of youth
Are marooned in mundane undertows,
'Neath crushing breakers of the truth.

It entails great grit and effort
To possess far distant shore,
Life's beset with changing currents
That pulls stiff upon the oars.

Pursuing goals once thought as trivial,
Summoning strength beyond great pain,
With stormy rage wrung out of protest
To inundate and crest again.

Water Lilies
Toussaint River

Respite

Luminous liquid lilies
Lay languid on the loch,
As winnowing winds work wetland weeds,
And waves wash over rocks.

Sharp sounds of scattering seagulls
Surround the sheltered shore,
As enticing eve tide etchings
Engulf what was before.

Raptors race to random rookery
Reserved in ragged trees,
As bunched and bustling blackbird bands
Break bog bottom bristled reeds.

Calming chants of clamorous crickets
Conjure up the coming night,
As upland spars and underbrush
Usher unsung birds from flight.

Peaceful points of peeking pulsars,
Populate the polar sky,
As mundane and maddening movements
Mitigate and finally die.

To rest, to sleep, to dream.

Suicide

Sometimes in life
we cannot hide
From intrusive thoughts
of dark suicide.

When last rational logic
seems to run
To choosing a knife,
a poison, a gun.

Some folks are despondent,
others failing, some shamed,
For me it's all physical –
about the damn pain.

And the drugs they give,
your ills to quell,
Wrench body and soul
claiming their own hell.

Mortified of check'n out,
used up from hang'n back,
Find'n mysteries of life
in the old gun rack.

In the end there's only
one choice to make,
For you're singular author
of your future fate.

So I choose this life
with all of its hells,
For it's God's precious gift,
and it's here that I'll dwell.

Trace

In deepest woods there is a trace,
That leads the timid through this place.

Along this path o'er hills and streams,
All wonders of our God are seen.

Among the trees, the rocks, the glens,
Lay treasures still untouched by men.

And all we are, and hope to be,
Have sprung from roots 'neath these great trees.

Wood Lilies
Dr. L.J. Darr Memorial Wetland

Deliverance

Emerald seas of rippling winter wheat
undulate on windswept fields.
From sheltered forest bedding plots
brave bulbs their colors yield.

Silent stands of swaying wood lots
boast boughs bedecked in buds.
River flats grow flocking shorebirds,
as snowy egrets wade tidal mud.

Warm kiss of early springtime
has revived this slumbering land
And bestowed a long-sought promise
of timely grace and bounty grand.

From the ample of her bosom
Nature tends this struggling life,
Gently nurturing new arrivals
that she lifts toward the light.

From within her fertile body
flourishing flora spring to sight,
As lush plains shout colors vibrant
rendering gardens of delight.

Soft caress strokes life abundant,
from Nature's largess it will grow,
In Life's tryst with earthly mother
resplendent felicity she'll bestow.

New life will rise in unison
as each year begins anew,
And so it is, and so it's been,
and will 'til time is through.

PURCHASED

Warm up the barbie,
Break out the beer,
The Fourth of July
Is finally here.

Hang out the bunting,
Strike up the band,
Proclaim the great heroes
And the glories of our Land.

There's time for celebration,
Time for grand parades,
Take time to thank the Veterans
For the sacrifice they've made.

A Republic strong and struggling
For many turbulent years,
Forged hot and quenched with Freedom,
Paid for with blood, and tears.

Most things of worthy value
Are garnered at great price,
But neglect of obligations
Will diminish Liberty and Rights.

This grand Land of "We the People",
This light of hope for all to see,
This brave bastion of Democracy,
This sheltering shield of Liberty.

Haven

Beneath pleasing patch of tranquil pines
On summer days my soul reclines.

On pallet of the softest weave
No sounds of life or footfalls leave.

The hubbub of this life around
Is muffled in this sheltered ground.

Songs of birds perching conifers' crowns,
Dense needles devour as they sail down.

Wandering winds stroke fragrant pines
Titillate the sense and rest the mind.

To this humble haven you come alone,
To salvage peace before head'n home.

Canada Geese In Winter
Sandusky River

KRISTALNACHT

Subdued in chains of endless winter,
We despondent slaves of sunless keep,
Shanghaied to serve The Clipper,
From Alberta's fabled fleet.

Propelled on gusts of grinding fury
All lay low before stiff gales,
Arctic hell will breed the great beast
Whose frigid trek leaves crystal trails.

All time for now's suspended
When quilted clouds match pearl-gray lake,
On shore march gleaming giants
As glacial ice erupts and breaks.

Inland, once dancing rivers
Have slowed and come to rest.
Gusting flurries feather ice and earth
Hiding marks of river crest.

Fence rows engulfed in snow dunes,
Windswept fields catch fading light,
As life escapes the living,
So winter day will pass to night.

SUNDOWNERS

In the midst of broiling summer
An annual pilgrimage we'll take,
For a day of fun and frolic –
An excursion to Erie Lake.

Gathering gear and folding money,
Traveling north to Put-In-Bay,
My wife and I drink in the sites,
And dream of younger days.

Gone are times of skimpy swimsuits
That now sag on aging frames,
Once hot youth in quest of high times,
Find spectating not the same.

Engulfed in throngs of summer sailors
Upon the ferry deck we'll ride,
Next to muscled boys in search of conquests
Among the girls with corn-rowed ties.

As we slip into the moorings
'Tween rich boats and deep lagoons,
Joining legions cursed with Gaelic hides
That slowly morph to black moorons.

Swelling tides of knick-knack shoppers
Flood food joints where all's deep-fried,
To lose decorum to the decadent
As crowds queue up for winery rides.

Propelled through gaping porous portals
Of gaudy open-air saloons,
Primeval screams of rowdy rock bands
Lure sidewalk strutters to their doom.

From berthings at the harbor
Lounging boaters come and go,
Some as joiners, some as watchers,
Of this bodacious bacchanalian show.

In days past we'd make the last boat,
Or sometimes bunk there all night.
But be it age, or be it wisdom,
We're now sundown cruisers taking flight.

Drake
2003
Centerville,TN

Defined

Without wild game, the gun
becomes a weapon.
Without the hunter, the retriever
becomes a dog.
Without the waterfowler, the marsh
becomes a swamp.
Without the woodsman, the forest
becomes foreboding.
Without the hunt, men
become endangered.

Standing Tall At WTC

HERO

Before the day of Tumbling Towers
The term laid loosely on our lips,
Exalting gladiators of cereal box,
Or becoming brunt of pundit's quips.

It crowned strutting kings of celluloid
Who'd never seen a foreign war,
But seldom used in painting commoners
Who labored 'mongst the sick and poor.

Pale pretenders claim the mantle,
But can't cloak their shallow ways,
Just coveting it won't meet the price
When mounting costs can shorten days.

Curse this age of social soothsayers
Who've bled white our sacred words,
Dismissing stirrings of great passion
For tripe prattling of the absurd.

But in times like this we've come to find
That folks of grit are made not born,
With their acts of selfless sacrifice,
They've redefined American norms.

Panoramic

When born to stellar mountains,
Folks back home will wonder why
That you'd venture to the flatlands –
The sole excuse is endless sky.

Set upon the Great Lakes delta,
Propped above flat prairie land,
Rests the easel of the Master
That boldly renders epics grand.

On the ever-changing canvas
Traversing heaven's domed grand expanse,
Are melded hues of vibrant colors
That from celestial pallets dance.

In textured depth and luminescence
Billowing clouds hang on the winds,
And the grandeur of this masterpiece
Pulls your soul from deep within.

You've seen the glow of early mornings,
And dawn's stealing of the night,
Each day a different showing
That revives dull senses with delight.

Many days well spent in watching
And drinking in this wondrous art,
Each is better than the first time,
Each evening rails against the dark.

Great White Heron
Dr. L.J. Darr Memorial Wetland

Tempest

On changing winds my future's blown,
In clouds of flux where all's unknown.

Upon the gales of twisting fate
Thrash crumpled dreams to contemplate.

With coming age I clearly see
Many squandered bygone opportunities.

So in the race that's not yet done
Can I change my ways and not succumb?

I'll just lift my eyes to greater things,
And soar the heights on mended wings.

Cock Pheasant
Dr. L.J. Darr Memorial Wetland

Roosters

I caught a fleeting flash of color
upon the distant hedgerow screen,
After breaking brush for hours
'twas first movement that I'd seen.

My lab was busy work'n
switchgrass and cattail reeds,
Intent on fleeing quarry
that would amply meet our needs.

We pushed this field just hoping
some flushing game would show,
Together trudging tanglefoot
on the freshly fallen snow.

Weighed down by sweat-drenched clothing
and arm killing twelve-gauge gun,
Bent against the gusting frigid breeze
that seemed fleeing from the sun.

In time we gained far fence row
upon the drifted snow we found
Spur marks of scooting pheasants,
where their tail feathers dragged the ground.

My dog inhaled a snoot full
of this beguiling avian sign,
While threading thicket like a needle
down the knotty fence row spine.

Canine gained in animation
as she plodded towards field's end,
On wind direction and straight shooting
our current fortunes would depend.

Hound and hunter stepped more slowly
approaching looming corner post,
For it's the habit of the pheasants
to only fly when they're provoked.

As we closed in on last cover
trembling dog surged for the game,
Two cocks with hens leapt skyward
as I swung waiting gun to aim.

With quick blasts I felled the roosters
that folded wings and crumpled down,
A perfect day for fellow hunters
as dog retrieved the birds we'd found.

Growing

Thrusting!
Outstretched!
Reaching!
Oak's gnarled claws will scrape the sky.
Probing!
Burrowing!
Hell-bound!
Roots thru layered earth they'll fly.
Flightless!
Trapped!
Befuddled!
In the middle ground I'll lie.
Wishing!
Praying!
Weeping!
Of fickle fate in days gone by.
Courage!
Knowledge!
Wisdom!
Sure to find them if I try.
Bounty!
Promise!
Redemption!
Savior's blood
my   I'll
With   buy.

Surrender

Crescendoed calls of chanting croakers
Cascade upon the coming night,
As lordly bulls and leaping leopards lure
Lonesome lovers to licentious delights.

Liquid lunar luminescence
Laps upon the languid land,
Docile deer discard deep cover
To devour grass on downwind stands.

Pervasive peace propels this ritual
Performed in preordained display,
Whispering winds will whimper gently
When waiting dawn weans restless day.

Cattle

We wait upon disaster
Like dumb beast in butcher's stall,
Intent upon the bloody ax
And the horror of it all.

It's hard to see tomorrow
When you live just for today,
And the bleating of our protests
Reflects impotence and dismay.

To lamely claim that station
And accept the fatal blow,
Or refuse to change the future
Is a damn poor way to go.

Life isn't always easy,
And is sometimes downright hard,
But you can choose to be the butcher
Or that quivering sack of lard!

Duel

First saw his track on quagmire quest,
Now again in wind swept snow.
From the mammoth cleavage of the earth
He's a grand big buck, ya know?

Found hidden scrapes and tangled rubs
That he gashed on sapling branch.
To count him 'mongst the taken
Mustn't leave the plans to chance.

So I hunkered down in snowy swale
'Mong dank scented cotton balls,
A granite pose in hunter orange
To await his slight footfalls.

Deftly I would cross his trail
Beneath sight and all downwind,
To lay perfumed trail of willing doe
Sure the rut might interest him.

From the confines of the quiet stand
I await the coming fray,
With my gun held poised in frozen hands
To welcome whitetail on this day.

Two snorts from deepest thicket
Tell me the game is done,
Seems the master of this game of death
Winded me 'fore setting sun.

We'll postpone this match 'til next year
When deer and man confront their foe,
This monster buck will gain in stature,
And I'll try to smell more like a doe.

WHY?

Chug-a-lug some Rusty Nails,
Soon knees give out and vision fails.

Take many tokes of Mary Jane,
Soon world affairs will seem quite sane.

Puff myriad packs of Lucky Strikes,
Soon gag and cough into the night.

Just dally with strange ladies much,
Soon wince to feel the surgeon's touch.

Sup heartily on the rich cuisine,
Soon girth expands to great extremes.

Seduced by love of greed and speed,
Soon priest or doctor you might need.

Great misspent youth where lusts are rife,
Soon brings us low or costs our life.

In age and wisdom all's chosen well,
But we'd chuck it quick to raise some hell.

Canada Goose Family
Dr. L.J. Darr Memorial Wetland

CURRENTS

Rushing egrets claim their night roosts
In stark barren willow trees.
Soon twinkling clones of ebbing sun
Will sprout on twilight breeze.

Goose will fetch the fuzzy goslings
Deftly stashed in grass'n dock,
To raft in shelter of the river
For it's the nighttime of the fox.

All the hustle and the bustle that
Comes in changing Nature's shift,
Brings a moment of reflection
Into which the soul might drift.

Like the geese in search of safety
Upon wide river's flow,
Sometimes trusting in the currents
When life has someplace else to go.

So embrace the fear of floundering
For the fox is far behind,
Cast all upon the waters
And hope the fates be kind.

On The Edge

Each is a sum of the whole
Yet distinction is drawn from the parts.

More readily defined by its form,
Too frequently recognized only by function.

Preserved as a grand compliment to the other
But rooted in stark contrast to its Gemini.

Night's existence is only gained by passing
And the day's identity is in its own demise.

Life's beauty rests in simple balances.
Uncomprehendingly,
we live only in the outlines.

Snapping Turtle
Dr. L.J. Darr Memorial Wetland

Turtle

I surprised her on the dike top
One balmy summer day,
Far from marsh's muddy haven
In dry ground her brood to lay.

This mammoth armored snapper
Spanned a foot and more in length,
Risking all for procreation,
At nature's urging she'd been sent.

Leathered pearls in great profusion
Tumbled in a gouged out trench,
Back-filled with labored motions
Offering future young but scant defense.

Great efforts to disguise her work
From the hungry beasts around,
The struggling titan deftly glides
Her shell o'er softly piled mound.

Lacking all that's thought maternal,
And with her reptilian duties done,
She quickly sought the friendly bog
With labored strides in ungainly run.

Left behind are hopes of hatchlings
That might join her in the fall,
When the pearls will turn to turtles,
Count them many, count them small.

The Bones of Innocence
Aftermath of the WTC Sept. 11, 2001

Been There

On the cusp of conflagration,
Days before the war birds fly,
Some in panic, some reflecting,
Mulling thoughts sane men deny.

There's a fear of what will follow,
Some quick prayers for heavenly shield;
All the chattering of the statesmen
Has yet much good to yield.

No one really wants to be there,
No one wants their own to go,
No one gives substantial answers
If it's a righteous path, or no.

With burning eyes from New York pyres
That dispelled complacent sleep,
We must gird against assassins
And willing company that they keep.

Denied an ax the hand's less frightful,
Deprived of shelter soon threats will fade,
Bold resolve shores up the timid
Amongst the allies that we've made.

With blind eyes we've read the present
Garnering freedom at frugal price,
Face it now and costs are daunting,
Be it wealth or loss of life.

We're a nation born in tumult
That's met the call for most our life,
If you think the future's different
You may never get it right.

Ballville Dam
Fremont, OH

Sandusky Passing

Last week I passed an old friend's grave,
It was snow blown and etched in time.
The stillness of the resting place
Was surreal and quite sublime.

There lay the corpse of old Sandusky,
An awesome river feeding treacherous bay,
Once the life-blood of the Great Black Swamp
That was northwest Ohio in early days.

The river's life had stopped this winter
When the temperate weather had fled south,
And gentle water flows froze solid
From headwaters to it's mouth.

Like the wound that won't heal over
At the rocks 'neath Ballville Dam
The cadaver bleeds pools of moisture
Despite the killing Winter's plan.

Like mourners at a funeral
Waterfowl flocked to pay respects,
To congregate 'round fonts of water
Perched on ice with scrunched-down necks.

Since then first blush of springtime
Has revived this terminal case,
New life surged 'neath the surface
And took ice flows from this place.

With the cresting of the river
Swift flotsam rides on mocha waves,
Spring's supplicants sing hallelujah
For Sandusky's risen from the grave.

Sprinters

A singular harbinger of Spring,
Brightly clad and extravagantly shod,
Huffing hosannas in chorus
As they worship the warming rays.
Vanquishing the last despondent Winter walkers
These phantoms of Spandex
Glide above the paths,
Staking their claims
To the winding threads of asphalt trails.
Their rites are enacted in youthful vigor
While discounting the beauty of their stage.
Performing physical acts of great denial
Questing only shifting goals
And hollow victories,
Soon delusion whispers lies of immortality.
Their changing surroundings are ignored,
Nature's cycles and axioms are unlearned.
Runners in a competition with no winners,
All contests conclude
When runners place, not win,
For the finish line has been harshly drawn.

Red Winged Blackbird
Magee Marsh

WHISPERINGS

I often sensed the Lord's displeasure
When I lived life and didn't care.
Frequently adding to His anguish,
Driving Him to great despair.

For most my life I've turned away
When He offered helping hands,
Sometimes wading on in disbelief
Or flat denying His grand plan.

I was a self-assured, a cut above,
And sole master of my fate;
No task in life beyond my reach,
No admission seemed too great.

He waited while I had my run
Destroying body, soul, and mind;
When I finally wept and begged for Him
To my entreaties he was kind.

What was the thing He saw in me,
That elicits this boundless love?
To stay with me as I spurned His ways
And His whisperings from above?

Some things in life I'll never know,
Some things I'll leave undone,
But in my heart there's inner peace
Since I've welcomed God's great Son.

Chukar

Those troublesome Chukar,

Most my good shots they duck-ar,

To bag'm takes luck-ar.

Wedding Feast

Draped in vestments of a cruel wake
Reposed last season's gay consort,
While the withered face of sleeping earth
Sports frozen mask of last resort.

From the blanket of the snow fields
Soon will rise the lately wed,
Who reflects new health and vigor
Like spry bride in marriage bed.

In great rapture of the living
All new life will rise as one,
Soon driven to competing
For warm affections of the sun.

All await the future coming
In the earth, the sea, the sky;
Snatching promise of deliverance
From the jaws of death's demise.

In anticipation of the hopeful
Gathered 'round for life's great feast,
We humbly beg for Spring's resurgence
Renewing flora, fowl, and beast.

Shooter

At the crusty age of eight years
I first took my son to hunt,
To walk the fields with rough-hewn men,
Four burly guys, two dogs, one runt.

Fast imbued in great traditions
Honing hunting skills and more,
He took to live'n like a red man,
Gaining gun skills and outdoor lore.

The boy first garnered goose that winter
Stradl'n a field blind's wobbly seat,
To earn the moniker of "Shooter"
From friends who'd seen his awesome feat.

Schooled in the wily ways of waterfowl,
Their flights, their shapes, their calls;
I was his guide to upland creatures
And the thrill of hunting for them all.

In Nature's grace he's grown to manhood
And kept these passions in his heart.
In the early years I've lead the way,
Now I'm infirmed and he must start.

In these days afield together
It's his task to lug the gear,
And in turn he shows great patience
For his guide of yesteryear.

Darr Carp Festival
Bobby Aikman
May 19, 2001

Fisher King

When it comes to knowing how to fish,
Some really do, and others wish.

No matter how they come equipped,
Some limit out and others quit.

There's some who with the fish converse,
And others plagued by Neptune's curse.

Long-time I've known the Fisher King,
The angler's life's been Bobby's thing.

He always knows where fish will hide,
In Lake Erie's depths or stream's bank sides.

He knows just how to tie the knots,
And choose the lures from what he's got.

He's master of the rod and reel,
Fish can't resist be'n his next meal.

Dervish

Framed in uprights of my back door
Awaits a weathered maple tree.
    Just last month 'twas stark and barren
With outstretched branches you could see.

In the waning days of autumn
It had shed its summer dress,
    And had stood there like a sentinel
To gain pause from winter's crest.

Now unfurling leaves of springtime
Paper o'er the gaping holes,
    To catch wind gusts of open prairie
While close-packed pines pitch and roll.

Soon the graceful dancing limb lengths
Move like dervish on the breeze,
    Dispelling last harsh thoughts of winter
As mellow summer takes its ease.

Thunderhead

In surrealistic streams of silence
Stout hearts slack to slow stand-still,
Seeking solid sorts of shelter
From surging squalls of early Spring.

Long nights are lost in loneliness
As luminous lightening laced the land,
Lunging lances of the lumbering light
Lash at looming loch and loam.

At will the tumult tears this tract,
Torrents throw their thunderous threat,
Through thatched trees 'long troubled trails
Tingling terror trounced and tread.

In quarried quays of quenching quiet
Quadrupeds're quickly quelled,
While in quagmires flapping quackers quest
Their quarters in marshland queues.

Whippoorwills all wet and wild-eyed
Winged to weeping-willow warrens,
Wiley warblers wrap in feathered wisps
Wrestle wind to welcome warmth.

Calming currents claim a cool caress
Consoling consternated and confused,
Culling creatures from close cover
When tempest's caldron will conclude.

Evening's End

Stilted shapes of scattered seagulls
Securely set on shifting shoals,
Embossed upon the switch-grass skeins
Sand entrenched on sheltering shore.

Pursuing last rich rays of evening
Lengthening shadows claim their due,
In the final gasp of daylight
Before struggling day is through.

Flocks flee the furthest feeding-fields
In forced march across the sky,
From the sanctuary of their daytime lairs,
Nighttime nibblers nimbly rise.

Intent upon the final act,
Creatures come and creatures go,
Oblivious to stark ethereal shift
As lingering shadows crest and flow.

Dr. John and Friend
Dr. John Scharding
Colorado Elk Hunt

Snoozer

He's Elmore's own, vet Doctor John,
Goes hunting elk in West's great beyond.

Each year he scales Colorado's heights
In search of bulls both day and night.

This year the hunt was mighty slim,
The drought dried grass, the forest thin.

But still he searched the draws and climbed
From valley floor to high tree line.

Nowhere this year could elk be found
In poplar stands or crag's high ground.

Many days of fruitless search were spent,
John gave up the hunt to return to tent.

As Doctor John crossed last ridge line
He beheld a sight that was so sublime.

Leaning upright 'gainst a poplar stand
Stood snoozing elk sporting rack so grand.

Hard tell'n then who was more surprised,
As hunter nudged elk to open his eyes.

Forgoing visions of the classic kill,
This meat hunter hip shot his bag to fill.

The great secret that this veterinarian knew,
Sleeping elk are relaxed, and easier to chew.

Resignation

The night sky is draped and churning
With billowing rain clouds it's festooned,
A mosaic swiftly moving
Impaled on iridescent harvest moon.

A chill has cloaked the evening
Driving swarming birds to rest,
Leaving whisperings of close Winter
When Fall has gathered in her best.

No one hears the fleeing Summer
As she swiftly passes by,
Drunk with ease we'll pause the great feast
And with foreboding watch the sky.

Discounting clues of shifting textures
And night's stealing of the day,
Betrayed by nature's frigid countenance
As patch-worked heavens turn somber gray.

All the comeliness of Summer
Will soon disappear with time,
Becoming mourners of her passing
Resigned to offerings less sublime.

China Moon

A China moon is still suspended
In crisp morning's teal blue sky,
It sets the tone for Winter's coming
As heavy frost on green grass lies.

In ivory bisque the orb is painted,
Sculpt upon a languid dawn,
Stark death-mask of passing Autumn
Awaiting Winter's covering storms.

Stirring birds rise much more slowly
As they soar in heaven's space,
Crimson leaves have left the great trees
That for years the river graced.

In tortured throes of passing over
All the seasons will converge,
Bravely giving of their last breath
Until only Winter's voice is heard.

Digger

Not hard tell'n where his burrow's at,
That dike destroy'n elusive muskrat.

He chews through all the marsh I built
To drain my ponds leave'n deep mud'n silt.

If he'll be lured to box trap cage,
That 'rat and kin won't see old age.

See'ns Believe'n

Show me a man
                  that has never failed,
And I'll show you
                  one lucky bloke.

Show me the glib-tongue
                  who says it all right,
And I'll pick out the man
                  that's not spoke.

Show me a man
                  who's never known fear,
I'll contend that
                  his reason's quite dead.

Show me a man
                  who's at peace with his wife,
And I'll show you
                  a eunuch in bed.

Show me the guy
                  who'll save me from myself,

Sure his soul
        will be twisted and mean.

Show me a man
        who has never known doubt,
And I'll show you
        one ego supreme.

Just show me someone
        who's not always sure,
But will give you
        the best that they've got.

You can count on the fact
        they'll do what they say,
And be principled
        more times than not.

Blue Winged Teal
Magee Marsh

Teal

Meandering gusts of Autumn breezes
Surf upon the cattail fronds,
Delivering flights of stealthy fliers
That clip the dike tops of my pond.

Devoid of sound they are upon you,
Betrayed by distant muffled splash,
Or the flash of wing patch vibrant
Of teal-blue streak that whistles past.

They're the early morning phantoms
That haunt the marsh's waking time,
On nimble wing they prove elusive
Seeking sheltering sedges 'round my blind.

All the blue wing and the green wing
That graze bog-bottom marshy floor,
They ply the mists of early season
And dissipate in first hard frost.

Tess
2003

Grief

Stuggl'n hard since my hound has passed,
I swore that Tess would be my last.

The bond ran deep 'tween dog and man,
A cherished gift the hunt demands.

Fall season's come, won't be the same,
Old memories glow amongst the pain.

I'll search for pups, but none will do,
For me and Tess the hunt is through.

All seasons change and so must I,
Sure I'll miss my friend until I die.

Conclusion

Will it be here in the future? That is the question that always comes to mind when we think about America's wild outdoors.

We are a nation blessed with what was once thought of as an endless bounty of natural resources and natural habitat. When asked, most Americans say they are conservationists and want to see our wealth of habitat and native species supported, maintained, and bequeathed to our future generations as a robust and vibrant heritage. Unfortunately, the effort at pursuing this goal has yet to be universally supported.

We have established many state and federal organizations to give direction and financial support through our tax dollars. Preservation organizations such as the Sierra Club and the Nature Conservancy have added political lobbying and funding for habitat acquisitions in environmentally critical areas. Sportsman's organizations have contributed funding and sweat equity to obtaining and restoring habitat, as well as stocking and wildlife propagation programs at a grass-roots level. One of the most critical contributions come from the hunters and fishermen that have contributed millions of dollars through the investment of the user fees from their annual license purchases that are directly invested in propagation, purchase, and habitat restoration.

The part of the equation that is missing is *you*! If the next generation of Americans is to benefit by inheriting a pristine wild outdoors, every one of us has to work to make that happen. Please get involved today, and share in the beauty and the grandeur of our Nation's wild outdoors.

About The Author

It seems only yesterday when my wife and I fled the crowded neighborhoods of Philadelphia in search of a new career and our first real home as newly-weds. It was our first great adventure together away from the provincial enclaves of the East Coast, and the sheltering protection of extended family. It was a real stretch for city kids like us adjusting to the rural setting of northwest Ohio, but our new neighbors in Fremont were gracious in helping us settle into the community.

And oh ...there was *The Lake*. Erie was the prize that we still marvel at today. Two hundred years ago this part of the country was known as the Great Black Swamp, and was the last part of Ohio settled by the European immigrants. Today it is still an area of meandering rivers, creeks, and placid lakefront.

Over the years our family grew by the addition of three great kids, and our grey hair increased exponentially. During our early years in Fremont my career as a manufacturing manager advanced, and my circle of friends grew to include the members of the Oak Harbor Conservation Club. Many days were spent in the company of these folks ranging the fields for upland game, or sitting in a duck blind swapping stories about our dogs while hunting waterfowl.

In July 1994 my life took an ugly turn; I became a cancer survivor. The downward spiral continued in January 1995 when I became totally disabled with Chronic Fatigue Syndrome and Fibromyalgia. Life as I knew it ceased to exist, and today I am still struggling to come back from the abyss.

Though faced with this life-changing challenge God sustained me with limitless support from friends and family, and my undiminished passion for the wild outdoors. My poetry reflects this continuing journey.

Just as each moment of greatness contains the seeds of its own destruction, every tragedy overcome enhances the living.

Printed in the United States
19086LVS00002B/1-102